DEDICATIO

For all CNC Programmers, Operators and Engineers

CNC LOG BOOK

TO MAKE OUR WORK EVEN BETTER.

Galas Products
★★★★★

THANKS FOR YOUR PURCHASE AND SUPPORT

LEAVE A COMMENT AND RATING.

**IF YOU FIND THIS DIARY HELPFUL,
PLEASE SHARE IT WITH OTHERS.**

THIS WILL HELP US CREATE MORE PROJECTS

IF YOU NEED MORE STUFF CHECK AUTHOR:

CNC ASSIST

ON AMAZON

Galas Products

★★★★★

NAME

SURNAME

ADRESS

PHONE NUMBER

E-MAIL

PROJECT DATA

· · · · · · ✤ · · · · · · ·

···

PROJECT OVERVIEW

PART NAME:

PART NUMBER:

MATERIAL:

MACHINING DETAILS

MACHINE:

PROGRAM NO:

REQUIREMENTS / CLAMPING

MEASURING TOOLS AND OTHER COMMENTS

TOOLS

	TOOL NAME / INSERTS		TOOLING SYSTEMS		OFFSET / PARAMETERS	
1						☐
2						☐
3						☐
4						☐
5						☐
6						☐
7						☐
8						☐
9						☐
10						☐
11						☐
12						☐
13						☐
14						☐
15						☐

PROJECT DATA

········ ❖ ········

···

PROJECT OVERVIEW

PART NAME: _____

PART NUMBER: _____

MATERIAL: _____

MACHINING DETAILS

MACHINE: _____

PROGRAM NO: _____

_____

REQUIREMENTS / CLAMPING

_____

_____

_____

_____

MEASURING TOOLS AND OTHER COMMENTS

_____

_____

_____

···

·····················
···
···

TOOLS

	TOOL NAME / INSERTS		TOOLING SYSTEMS		OFFSET / PARAMETERS	
1						☐
2						☐
3						☐
4						☐
5						☐
6						☐
7						☐
8						☐
9						☐
10						☐
11						☐
12						☐
13						☐
14						☐
15						☐

PROJECT DATA

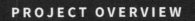

PROJECT OVERVIEW

PART NAME:

PART NUMBER:

MATERIAL:

MACHINING DETAILS

MACHINE:

PROGRAM NO:

REQUIREMENTS / CLAMPING

MEASURING TOOLS AND OTHER COMMENTS

TOOLS

	TOOL NAME / INSERTS		TOOLING SYSTEMS		OFFSET / PARAMETERS	
1						☐
2						☐
3						☐
4						☐
5						☐
6						☐
7						☐
8						☐
9						☐
10						☐
11						☐
12						☐
13						☐
14						☐
15						☐

PROJECT DATA

•••••• ❖ ••••••

••

PROJECT OVERVIEW

PART NAME:

PART NUMBER:

MATERIAL:

MACHINING DETAILS

MACHINE:

PROGRAM NO:

REQUIREMENTS / CLAMPING

MEASURING TOOLS AND OTHER COMMENTS

TOOLS

	TOOL NAME / INSERTS		TOOLING SYSTEMS		OFFSET / PARAMETERS	
1						☐
2						☐
3						☐
4						☐
5						☐
6						☐
7						☐
8						☐
9						☐
10						☐
11						☐
12						☐
13						☐
14						☐
15						☐

PROJECT DATA

•••••• ❖ ••••••

PROJECT OVERVIEW

PART NAME:

PART NUMBER:

MATERIAL:

MACHINING DETAILS

MACHINE:

PROGRAM NO:

REQUIREMENTS / CLAMPING

MEASURING TOOLS AND OTHER COMMENTS

TOOLS

	TOOL NAME / INSERTS		TOOLING SYSTEMS		OFFSET / PARAMETERS	
1						☐
2						☐
3						☐
4						☐
5						☐
6						☐
7						☐
8						☐
9						☐
10						☐
11						☐
12						☐
13						☐
14						☐
15						☐

PROJECT DATA

.... ❖ ....

....

PROJECT OVERVIEW

PART NAME: _____

PART NUMBER: _____

MATERIAL: _____

MACHINING DETAILS

MACHINE: _____

PROGRAM NO: _____

_____

REQUIREMENTS / CLAMPING

_____

_____

_____

_____

MEASURING TOOLS AND OTHER COMMENTS

_____

_____

_____

_____

....

....

....

TOOLS

	TOOL NAME / INSERTS		TOOLING SYSTEMS		OFFSET / PARAMETERS	
1						☐
2						☐
3						☐
4						☐
5						☐
6						☐
7						☐
8						☐
9						☐
10						☐
11						☐
12						☐
13						☐
14						☐
15						☐

PROJECT DATA

•••••• ❖ ••••••

PROJECT OVERVIEW

PART NAME:

PART NUMBER:

MATERIAL:

MACHINING DETAILS

MACHINE:

PROGRAM NO:

REQUIREMENTS / CLAMPING

MEASURING TOOLS AND OTHER COMMENTS

TOOLS

	TOOL NAME / INSERTS		TOOLING SYSTEMS		OFFSET / PARAMETERS	
1						☐
2						☐
3						☐
4						☐
5						☐
6						☐
7						☐
8						☐
9						☐
10						☐
11						☐
12						☐
13						☐
14						☐
15						☐

PROJECT DATA

PROJECT OVERVIEW

PART NAME:

PART NUMBER:

MATERIAL:

MACHINING DETAILS

MACHINE:

PROGRAM NO:

REQUIREMENTS / CLAMPING

MEASURING TOOLS AND OTHER COMMENTS

TOOLS

	TOOL NAME / INSERTS		TOOLING SYSTEMS		OFFSET / PARAMETERS	
1						☐
2						☐
3						☐
4						☐
5						☐
6						☐
7						☐
8						☐
9						☐
10						☐
11						☐
12						☐
13						☐
14						☐
15						☐

PROJECT DATA

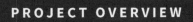

....

PROJECT OVERVIEW

PART NAME: _____

PART NUMBER: _____

MATERIAL: _____

MACHINING DETAILS

MACHINE: _____

PROGRAM NO: _____

_____

REQUIREMENTS / CLAMPING

_____

_____

_____

MEASURING TOOLS AND OTHER COMMENTS

_____

_____

_____

....

....

....

TOOLS

	TOOL NAME / INSERTS		TOOLING SYSTEMS		OFFSET / PARAMETERS	
1						☐
2						☐
3						☐
4						☐
5						☐
6						☐
7						☐
8						☐
9						☐
10						☐
11						☐
12						☐
13						☐
14						☐
15						☐

PROJECT DATA

•••••• ✤ ••••••

••••••••••••••••••••••••••••••

PROJECT OVERVIEW

PART NAME: _____

PART NUMBER: _____

MATERIAL: _____

MACHINING DETAILS

MACHINE: _____

PROGRAM NO: _____

_____

REQUIREMENTS / CLAMPING

_____

_____

_____

_____

MEASURING TOOLS AND OTHER COMMENTS

_____

_____

_____

••••••••••••••••••••••

••••••••••••••••••••••

•••••••••••• ••••••••••••••••••••••

TOOLS

	TOOL NAME / INSERTS		TOOLING SYSTEMS		OFFSET / PARAMETERS	
1						☐
2						☐
3						☐
4						☐
5						☐
6						☐
7						☐
8						☐
9						☐
10						☐
11						☐
12						☐
13						☐
14						☐
15						☐

PROJECT DATA

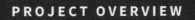

PROJECT OVERVIEW

PART NAME:

PART NUMBER:

MATERIAL:

MACHINING DETAILS

MACHINE:

PROGRAM NO:

REQUIREMENTS / CLAMPING

MEASURING TOOLS AND OTHER COMMENTS

TOOLS

	TOOL NAME / INSERTS		TOOLING SYSTEMS		OFFSET / PARAMETERS	
1						☐
2						☐
3						☐
4						☐
5						☐
6						☐
7						☐
8						☐
9						☐
10						☐
11						☐
12						☐
13						☐
14						☐
15						☐

PROJECT DATA

••••••• ❖ •••••••

....

PROJECT OVERVIEW

PART NAME: _____

PART NUMBER: _____

MATERIAL: _____

MACHINING DETAILS

MACHINE: _____

PROGRAM NO: _____

_____

REQUIREMENTS / CLAMPING

_____

_____

_____

MEASURING TOOLS AND OTHER COMMENTS

_____

_____

_____

....

....

....

....

TOOLS

	TOOL NAME / INSERTS		TOOLING SYSTEMS		OFFSET / PARAMETERS	
1						☐
2						☐
3						☐
4						☐
5						☐
6						☐
7						☐
8						☐
9						☐
10						☐
11						☐
12						☐
13						☐
14						☐
15						☐

PROJECT DATA

...... ❖ ....

....

PROJECT OVERVIEW

PART NAME: _____

PART NUMBER: _____

MATERIAL: _____

MACHINING DETAILS

MACHINE: _____

PROGRAM NO: _____

_____

REQUIREMENTS / CLAMPING

_____

_____

_____

MEASURING TOOLS AND OTHER COMMENTS

_____

_____

_____

TOOLS

	TOOL NAME / INSERTS		TOOLING SYSTEMS		OFFSET / PARAMETERS	
1						☐
2						☐
3						☐
4						☐
5						☐
6						☐
7						☐
8						☐
9						☐
10						☐
11						☐
12						☐
13						☐
14						☐
15						☐

PROJECT DATA

.... ❖ ....

....

PROJECT OVERVIEW

PART NAME: _____

PART NUMBER: _____

MATERIAL: _____

MACHINING DETAILS

MACHINE: _____

PROGRAM NO: _____

_____

REQUIREMENTS / CLAMPING

_____

_____

_____

MEASURING TOOLS AND OTHER COMMENTS

_____

_____

_____

TOOLS

	TOOL NAME / INSERTS		TOOLING SYSTEMS		OFFSET / PARAMETERS	
1						☐
2						☐
3						☐
4						☐
5						☐
6						☐
7						☐
8						☐
9						☐
10						☐
11						☐
12						☐
13						☐
14						☐
15						☐

PROJECT DATA

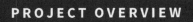

··

PROJECT OVERVIEW

PART NAME: _____

PART NUMBER: _____

MATERIAL: _____

MACHINING DETAILS

MACHINE: _____

PROGRAM NO: _____

_____

REQUIREMENTS / CLAMPING

_____

_____

_____

MEASURING TOOLS AND OTHER COMMENTS

_____

_____

_____

··

··

··

TOOLS

	TOOL NAME / INSERTS		TOOLING SYSTEMS		OFFSET / PARAMETERS	
1						☐
2						☐
3						☐
4						☐
5						☐
6						☐
7						☐
8						☐
9						☐
10						☐
11						☐
12						☐
13						☐
14						☐
15						☐

PROJECT DATA

.... ❖ ....

....

PROJECT OVERVIEW

PART NAME: _____

PART NUMBER: _____

MATERIAL: _____

MACHINING DETAILS

MACHINE: _____

PROGRAM NO: _____

_____

REQUIREMENTS / CLAMPING

_____

_____

_____

MEASURING TOOLS AND OTHER COMMENTS

_____

_____

_____

TOOLS

	TOOL NAME / INSERTS		TOOLING SYSTEMS		OFFSET / PARAMETERS	
1						☐
2						☐
3						☐
4						☐
5						☐
6						☐
7						☐
8						☐
9						☐
10						☐
11						☐
12						☐
13						☐
14						☐
15						☐

PROJECT DATA

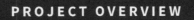

PROJECT OVERVIEW

PART NAME:

PART NUMBER:

MATERIAL:

MACHINING DETAILS

MACHINE:

PROGRAM NO:

REQUIREMENTS / CLAMPING

MEASURING TOOLS AND OTHER COMMENTS

TOOLS

	TOOL NAME / INSERTS		TOOLING SYSTEMS		OFFSET / PARAMETERS	
1						☐
2						☐
3						☐
4						☐
5						☐
6						☐
7						☐
8						☐
9						☐
10						☐
11						☐
12						☐
13						☐
14						☐
15						☐

PROJECT DATA

•••••• ❖ ••••••

....

PROJECT OVERVIEW

PART NAME: _____

PART NUMBER: _____

MATERIAL: _____

MACHINING DETAILS

MACHINE: _____

PROGRAM NO: _____

_____

REQUIREMENTS / CLAMPING

_____

_____

_____

MEASURING TOOLS AND OTHER COMMENTS

_____

_____

_____

TOOLS

	TOOL NAME / INSERTS		TOOLING SYSTEMS		OFFSET / PARAMETERS	
1						☐
2						☐
3						☐
4						☐
5						☐
6						☐
7						☐
8						☐
9						☐
10						☐
11						☐
12						☐
13						☐
14						☐
15						☐

PROJECT DATA

•••••• ❖ ••••••

••••••••••••••••••••••••••••••••

PROJECT OVERVIEW

PART NAME:

PART NUMBER:

MATERIAL:

MACHINING DETAILS

MACHINE:

PROGRAM NO:

REQUIREMENTS / CLAMPING

MEASURING TOOLS AND OTHER COMMENTS

TOOLS

	TOOL NAME / INSERTS		TOOLING SYSTEMS		OFFSET / PARAMETERS	
1						☐
2						☐
3						☐
4						☐
5						☐
6						☐
7						☐
8						☐
9						☐
10						☐
11						☐
12						☐
13						☐
14						☐
15						☐

PROJECT DATA

························ ❖ ········

··

PROJECT OVERVIEW

PART NAME:

PART NUMBER:

MATERIAL:

MACHINING DETAILS

MACHINE:

PROGRAM NO:

REQUIREMENTS / CLAMPING

MEASURING TOOLS AND OTHER COMMENTS

TOOLS

	TOOL NAME / INSERTS		TOOLING SYSTEMS		OFFSET / PARAMETERS	
1						☐
2						☐
3						☐
4						☐
5						☐
6						☐
7						☐
8						☐
9						☐
10						☐
11						☐
12						☐
13						☐
14						☐
15						☐

PROJECT DATA

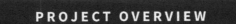

PROJECT OVERVIEW

PART NAME:

PART NUMBER:

MATERIAL:

MACHINING DETAILS

MACHINE:

PROGRAM NO:

REQUIREMENTS / CLAMPING

MEASURING TOOLS AND OTHER COMMENTS

TOOLS

	TOOL NAME / INSERTS		TOOLING SYSTEMS		OFFSET / PARAMETERS	
1						☐
2						☐
3						☐
4						☐
5						☐
6						☐
7						☐
8						☐
9						☐
10						☐
11						☐
12						☐
13						☐
14						☐
15						☐

PROJECT DATA

•••••• ❖ ••••••

....

PROJECT OVERVIEW

PART NAME:

PART NUMBER:

MATERIAL:

MACHINING DETAILS

MACHINE:

PROGRAM NO:

REQUIREMENTS / CLAMPING

MEASURING TOOLS AND OTHER COMMENTS

TOOLS

	TOOL NAME / INSERTS		TOOLING SYSTEMS		OFFSET / PARAMETERS	
1						☐
2						☐
3						☐
4						☐
5						☐
6						☐
7						☐
8						☐
9						☐
10						☐
11						☐
12						☐
13						☐
14						☐
15						☐

PROJECT DATA

PROJECT OVERVIEW

PART NAME:

PART NUMBER:

MATERIAL:

MACHINING DETAILS

MACHINE:

PROGRAM NO:

REQUIREMENTS / CLAMPING

MEASURING TOOLS AND OTHER COMMENTS

TOOLS

	TOOL NAME / INSERTS		TOOLING SYSTEMS		OFFSET / PARAMETERS	
1						
2						
3						
4						
5						
6						
7						
8						
9						
10						
11						
12						
13						
14						
15						

PROJECT DATA

•••••• ❖ ••••••

....

PROJECT OVERVIEW

PART NAME:

PART NUMBER:

MATERIAL:

MACHINING DETAILS

MACHINE:

PROGRAM NO:

REQUIREMENTS / CLAMPING

MEASURING TOOLS AND OTHER COMMENTS

TOOLS

	TOOL NAME / INSERTS		TOOLING SYSTEMS		OFFSET / PARAMETERS	
1						☐
2						☐
3						☐
4						☐
5						☐
6						☐
7						☐
8						☐
9						☐
10						☐
11						☐
12						☐
13						☐
14						☐
15						☐

PROJECT DATA

· · · · · · · ❖ · · · · · · ·

PROJECT OVERVIEW

PART NAME:

PART NUMBER:

MATERIAL:

MACHINING DETAILS

MACHINE:

PROGRAM NO:

REQUIREMENTS / CLAMPING

MEASURING TOOLS AND OTHER COMMENTS

TOOLS

	TOOL NAME / INSERTS		TOOLING SYSTEMS		OFFSET / PARAMETERS	
1						☐
2						☐
3						☐
4						☐
5						☐
6						☐
7						☐
8						☐
9						☐
10						☐
11						☐
12						☐
13						☐
14						☐
15						☐

PROJECT DATA

•••••• ❖ ••••••

....

PROJECT OVERVIEW

PART NAME:

PART NUMBER:

MATERIAL:

MACHINING DETAILS

MACHINE:

PROGRAM NO:

REQUIREMENTS / CLAMPING

MEASURING TOOLS AND OTHER COMMENTS

TOOLS

	TOOL NAME / INSERTS		TOOLING SYSTEMS		OFFSET / PARAMETERS	
1						☐
2						☐
3						☐
4						☐
5						☐
6						☐
7						☐
8						☐
9						☐
10						☐
11						☐
12						☐
13						☐
14						☐
15						☐

PROJECT DATA

PROJECT OVERVIEW

PART NAME:

PART NUMBER:

MATERIAL:

MACHINING DETAILS

MACHINE:

PROGRAM NO:

REQUIREMENTS / CLAMPING

MEASURING TOOLS AND OTHER COMMENTS

TOOLS

	TOOL NAME / INSERTS		TOOLING SYSTEMS		OFFSET / PARAMETERS	
1						☐
2						☐
3						☐
4						☐
5						☐
6						☐
7						☐
8						☐
9						☐
10						☐
11						☐
12						☐
13						☐
14						☐
15						☐

PROJECT DATA

•••••• ❖ ••••••

···

PROJECT OVERVIEW

PART NAME: _____

PART NUMBER: _____

MATERIAL: _____

MACHINING DETAILS

MACHINE: _____

PROGRAM NO: _____

_____

REQUIREMENTS / CLAMPING

_____

_____

_____

_____

MEASURING TOOLS AND OTHER COMMENTS

_____

_____

_____

_____

TOOLS

	TOOL NAME / INSERTS		TOOLING SYSTEMS		OFFSET / PARAMETERS	
1						☐
2						☐
3						☐
4						☐
5						☐
6						☐
7						☐
8						☐
9						☐
10						☐
11						☐
12						☐
13						☐
14						☐
15						☐

PROJECT DATA

······ ❖ ······

··

PROJECT OVERVIEW

PART NAME: _____

PART NUMBER: _____

MATERIAL: _____

MACHINING DETAILS

MACHINE: _____

PROGRAM NO: _____

_____

REQUIREMENTS / CLAMPING

_____

_____

_____

_____

MEASURING TOOLS AND OTHER COMMENTS

_____

_____

_____

_____

··

··

··

··

TOOLS

	TOOL NAME / INSERTS		TOOLING SYSTEMS		OFFSET / PARAMETERS	
1						☐
2						☐
3						☐
4						☐
5						☐
6						☐
7						☐
8						☐
9						☐
10						☐
11						☐
12						☐
13						☐
14						☐
15						☐

PROJECT DATA

PROJECT OVERVIEW

PART NAME:

PART NUMBER:

MATERIAL:

MACHINING DETAILS

MACHINE:

PROGRAM NO:

REQUIREMENTS / CLAMPING

MEASURING TOOLS AND OTHER COMMENTS

TOOLS

	TOOL NAME / INSERTS		TOOLING SYSTEMS		OFFSET / PARAMETERS	
1						☐
2						☐
3						☐
4						☐
5						☐
6						☐
7						☐
8						☐
9						☐
10						☐
11						☐
12						☐
13						☐
14						☐
15						☐

PROJECT DATA

•••••• ❖ ••••••

....

PROJECT OVERVIEW

PART NAME:

PART NUMBER:

MATERIAL:

MACHINING DETAILS

MACHINE:

PROGRAM NO:

REQUIREMENTS / CLAMPING

MEASURING TOOLS AND OTHER COMMENTS

TOOLS

	TOOL NAME / INSERTS		TOOLING SYSTEMS		OFFSET / PARAMETERS	
1						☐
2						☐
3						☐
4						☐
5						☐
6						☐
7						☐
8						☐
9						☐
10						☐
11						☐
12						☐
13						☐
14						☐
15						☐

PROJECT DATA

•••••• ❖ ••••••

....

PROJECT OVERVIEW

PART NAME: _____

PART NUMBER: _____

MATERIAL: _____

MACHINING DETAILS

MACHINE: _____

PROGRAM NO: _____

_____

REQUIREMENTS / CLAMPING

_____

_____

_____

MEASURING TOOLS AND OTHER COMMENTS

_____

_____

_____

....

....

....

TOOLS

	TOOL NAME / INSERTS		TOOLING SYSTEMS		OFFSET / PARAMETERS	
1						☐
2						☐
3						☐
4						☐
5						☐
6						☐
7						☐
8						☐
9						☐
10						☐
11						☐
12						☐
13						☐
14						☐
15						☐

PROJECT DATA

.... ✣ ....

....

PROJECT OVERVIEW

PART NAME: _____

PART NUMBER: _____

MATERIAL: _____

MACHINING DETAILS

MACHINE: _____

PROGRAM NO: _____

_____

REQUIREMENTS / CLAMPING

_____

_____

_____

_____

MEASURING TOOLS AND OTHER COMMENTS

_____

_____

_____

_____

....

....

....

TOOLS

	TOOL NAME / INSERTS		TOOLING SYSTEMS		OFFSET / PARAMETERS	
1						
2						
3						
4						
5						
6						
7						
8						
9						
10						
11						
12						
13						
14						
15						

PROJECT DATA

······· ❖ ·······

....

PROJECT OVERVIEW

PART NAME: _____

PART NUMBER: _____

MATERIAL: _____

MACHINING DETAILS

MACHINE: _____

PROGRAM NO: _____

_____

REQUIREMENTS / CLAMPING

_____

_____

_____

_____

MEASURING TOOLS AND OTHER COMMENTS

_____

_____

_____

_____

TOOLS

	TOOL NAME / INSERTS		TOOLING SYSTEMS		OFFSET / PARAMETERS	
1						☐
2						☐
3						☐
4						☐
5						☐
6						☐
7						☐
8						☐
9						☐
10						☐
11						☐
12						☐
13						☐
14						☐
15						☐

PROJECT DATA

• • • • • • ❖ • • • • • • •

PROJECT OVERVIEW

PART NAME:

PART NUMBER:

MATERIAL:

MACHINING DETAILS

MACHINE:

PROGRAM NO:

REQUIREMENTS / CLAMPING

MEASURING TOOLS AND OTHER COMMENTS

TOOLS

	TOOL NAME / INSERTS		TOOLING SYSTEMS		OFFSET / PARAMETERS	
1						
2						
3						
4						
5						
6						
7						
8						
9						
10						
11						
12						
13						
14						
15						

PROJECT DATA

...... ❖ ......

....

PROJECT OVERVIEW

PART NAME:

PART NUMBER:

MATERIAL:

MACHINING DETAILS

MACHINE:

PROGRAM NO:

REQUIREMENTS / CLAMPING

MEASURING TOOLS AND OTHER COMMENTS

....

....

....

TOOLS

	TOOL NAME / INSERTS		TOOLING SYSTEMS		OFFSET / PARAMETERS	
1						☐
2						☐
3						☐
4						☐
5						☐
6						☐
7						☐
8						☐
9						☐
10						☐
11						☐
12						☐
13						☐
14						☐
15						☐

PROJECT DATA

•••••• ❖ ••••••

PROJECT OVERVIEW

PART NAME:

PART NUMBER:

MATERIAL:

MACHINING DETAILS

MACHINE:

PROGRAM NO:

REQUIREMENTS / CLAMPING

MEASURING TOOLS AND OTHER COMMENTS

TOOLS

	TOOL NAME / INSERTS		TOOLING SYSTEMS		OFFSET / PARAMETERS	
1						☐
2						☐
3						☐
4						☐
5						☐
6						☐
7						☐
8						☐
9						☐
10						☐
11						☐
12						☐
13						☐
14						☐
15						☐

PROJECT DATA

PROJECT OVERVIEW

PART NAME: _____

PART NUMBER: _____

MATERIAL: _____

MACHINING DETAILS

MACHINE: _____

PROGRAM NO: _____

_____

REQUIREMENTS / CLAMPING

_____

_____

_____

MEASURING TOOLS AND OTHER COMMENTS

_____

_____

_____

TOOLS

	TOOL NAME / INSERTS		TOOLING SYSTEMS		OFFSET / PARAMETERS	
1						
2						
3						
4						
5						
6						
7						
8						
9						
10						
11						
12						
13						
14						
15						

PROJECT DATA

.... ❖ ....

....

PROJECT OVERVIEW

PART NAME:

PART NUMBER:

MATERIAL:

MACHINING DETAILS

MACHINE:

PROGRAM NO:

REQUIREMENTS / CLAMPING

MEASURING TOOLS AND OTHER COMMENTS

....

....

....

....

....

TOOLS

	TOOL NAME / INSERTS		TOOLING SYSTEMS		OFFSET / PARAMETERS	
1						☐
2						☐
3						☐
4						☐
5						☐
6						☐
7						☐
8						☐
9						☐
10						☐
11						☐
12						☐
13						☐
14						☐
15						☐

PROJECT DATA

•••••• ❖ ••••••

··

PROJECT OVERVIEW

PART NAME: _____

PART NUMBER: _____

MATERIAL: _____

MACHINING DETAILS

MACHINE: _____

PROGRAM NO: _____

_____

REQUIREMENTS / CLAMPING

_____

_____

_____

MEASURING TOOLS AND OTHER COMMENTS

_____

_____

_____

····························

·················   ····························

TOOLS

	TOOL NAME / INSERTS		TOOLING SYSTEMS		OFFSET / PARAMETERS	
1						
2						
3						
4						
5						
6						
7						
8						
9						
10						
11						
12						
13						
14						
15						

PROJECT DATA

•••••• ❖ ••••••

....

PROJECT OVERVIEW

PART NAME:

PART NUMBER:

MATERIAL:

MACHINING DETAILS

MACHINE:

PROGRAM NO:

REQUIREMENTS / CLAMPING

MEASURING TOOLS AND OTHER COMMENTS

TOOLS

	TOOL NAME / INSERTS		TOOLING SYSTEMS		OFFSET / PARAMETERS	
1						☐
2						☐
3						☐
4						☐
5						☐
6						☐
7						☐
8						☐
9						☐
10						☐
11						☐
12						☐
13						☐
14						☐
15						☐

PROJECT DATA

· · · · · · · ❖ · · · · · · ·

· ·

PROJECT OVERVIEW

PART NAME: _____

PART NUMBER: _____

MATERIAL: _____

MACHINING DETAILS

MACHINE: _____

PROGRAM NO: _____

_____

REQUIREMENTS / CLAMPING

_____

_____

_____

_____

MEASURING TOOLS AND OTHER COMMENTS

_____

_____

_____

· ·

· ·

· · · · · · · · · · · · ·   ·

TOOLS

	TOOL NAME / INSERTS		TOOLING SYSTEMS		OFFSET / PARAMETERS	
1						☐
2						☐
3						☐
4						☐
5						☐
6						☐
7						☐
8						☐
9						☐
10						☐
11						☐
12						☐
13						☐
14						☐
15						☐

PROJECT DATA

•••••• ❖ ••••••

....

PROJECT OVERVIEW

PART NAME:

PART NUMBER:

MATERIAL:

MACHINING DETAILS

MACHINE:

PROGRAM NO:

REQUIREMENTS / CLAMPING

MEASURING TOOLS AND OTHER COMMENTS

....

....

....

TOOLS

	TOOL NAME / INSERTS		TOOLING SYSTEMS		OFFSET / PARAMETERS	
1						
2						
3						
4						
5						
6						
7						
8						
9						
10						
11						
12						
13						
14						
15						

PROJECT DATA

PROJECT OVERVIEW

PART NAME:

PART NUMBER:

MATERIAL:

MACHINING DETAILS

MACHINE:

PROGRAM NO:

REQUIREMENTS / CLAMPING

MEASURING TOOLS AND OTHER COMMENTS

TOOLS

	TOOL NAME / INSERTS		TOOLING SYSTEMS		OFFSET / PARAMETERS	
1						☐
2						☐
3						☐
4						☐
5						☐
6						☐
7						☐
8						☐
9						☐
10						☐
11						☐
12						☐
13						☐
14						☐
15						☐

PROJECT DATA

······ ❖ ······

....

PROJECT OVERVIEW

PART NAME: _____

PART NUMBER: _____

MATERIAL: _____

MACHINING DETAILS

MACHINE: _____

PROGRAM NO: _____

_____

REQUIREMENTS / CLAMPING

_____

_____

_____

_____

MEASURING TOOLS AND OTHER COMMENTS

_____

_____

_____

_____

....

....

....

TOOLS

	TOOL NAME / INSERTS		TOOLING SYSTEMS		OFFSET / PARAMETERS	
1						☐
2						☐
3						☐
4						☐
5						☐
6						☐
7						☐
8						☐
9						☐
10						☐
11						☐
12						☐
13						☐
14						☐
15						☐

PROJECT DATA

PROJECT OVERVIEW

PART NAME: _____

PART NUMBER: _____

MATERIAL: _____

MACHINING DETAILS

MACHINE: _____

PROGRAM NO: _____

_____

REQUIREMENTS / CLAMPING

_____

_____

_____

_____

MEASURING TOOLS AND OTHER COMMENTS

_____

_____

_____

TOOLS

	TOOL NAME / INSERTS		TOOLING SYSTEMS		OFFSET / PARAMETERS	
1						☐
2						☐
3						☐
4						☐
5						☐
6						☐
7						☐
8						☐
9						☐
10						☐
11						☐
12						☐
13						☐
14						☐
15						☐

PROJECT DATA

•••••• ❖ ••••••

....

PROJECT OVERVIEW

PART NAME: _____

PART NUMBER: _____

MATERIAL: _____

MACHINING DETAILS

MACHINE: _____

PROGRAM NO: _____

_____

REQUIREMENTS / CLAMPING

_____

_____

_____

_____

MEASURING TOOLS AND OTHER COMMENTS

_____

_____

_____

_____

....

....

....

TOOLS

	TOOL NAME / INSERTS		TOOLING SYSTEMS		OFFSET / PARAMETERS	
1						
2						
3						
4						
5						
6						
7						
8						
9						
10						
11						
12						
13						
14						
15						

PROJECT DATA

.... ❖ ....

....

PROJECT OVERVIEW

PART NAME: _____

PART NUMBER: _____

MATERIAL: _____

MACHINING DETAILS

MACHINE: _____

PROGRAM NO: _____

_____

REQUIREMENTS / CLAMPING

_____

_____

_____

_____

MEASURING TOOLS AND OTHER COMMENTS

_____

_____

_____

_____

....

....

TOOLS

	TOOL NAME / INSERTS		TOOLING SYSTEMS		OFFSET / PARAMETERS	
1						☐
2						☐
3						☐
4						☐
5						☐
6						☐
7						☐
8						☐
9						☐
10						☐
11						☐
12						☐
13						☐
14						☐
15						☐

PROJECT DATA

PROJECT OVERVIEW

PART NAME:

PART NUMBER:

MATERIAL:

MACHINING DETAILS

MACHINE:

PROGRAM NO:

REQUIREMENTS / CLAMPING

MEASURING TOOLS AND OTHER COMMENTS

TOOLS

	TOOL NAME / INSERTS		TOOLING SYSTEMS		OFFSET / PARAMETERS	
1						☐
2						☐
3						☐
4						☐
5						☐
6						☐
7						☐
8						☐
9						☐
10						☐
11						☐
12						☐
13						☐
14						☐
15						☐

PROJECT DATA

••••••• ❖ •••••••

....

PROJECT OVERVIEW

PART NAME: _____

PART NUMBER: _____

MATERIAL: _____

MACHINING DETAILS

MACHINE: _____

PROGRAM NO: _____

_____

REQUIREMENTS / CLAMPING

_____

_____

_____

_____

MEASURING TOOLS AND OTHER COMMENTS

_____

_____

_____

_____

....

....

....

TOOLS

	TOOL NAME / INSERTS		TOOLING SYSTEMS		OFFSET / PARAMETERS	
1						☐
2						☐
3						☐
4						☐
5						☐
6						☐
7						☐
8						☐
9						☐
10						☐
11						☐
12						☐
13						☐
14						☐
15						☐

PROJECT DATA

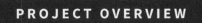

....

PROJECT OVERVIEW

PART NAME: _____

PART NUMBER: _____

MATERIAL: _____

MACHINING DETAILS

MACHINE: _____

PROGRAM NO: _____

_____

REQUIREMENTS / CLAMPING

_____

_____

_____

MEASURING TOOLS AND OTHER COMMENTS

_____

_____

_____

....

....

....

TOOLS

	TOOL NAME / INSERTS		TOOLING SYSTEMS		OFFSET / PARAMETERS	
1						☐
2						☐
3						☐
4						☐
5						☐
6						☐
7						☐
8						☐
9						☐
10						☐
11						☐
12						☐
13						☐
14						☐
15						☐

PROJECT DATA

••••••• ✤ •••••••

....

PROJECT OVERVIEW

PART NAME:

PART NUMBER:

MATERIAL:

MACHINING DETAILS

MACHINE:

PROGRAM NO:

REQUIREMENTS / CLAMPING

MEASURING TOOLS AND OTHER COMMENTS

....

....

....

....

TOOLS

	TOOL NAME / INSERTS		TOOLING SYSTEMS		OFFSET / PARAMETERS	
1						☐
2						☐
3						☐
4						☐
5						☐
6						☐
7						☐
8						☐
9						☐
10						☐
11						☐
12						☐
13						☐
14						☐
15						☐

PROJECT DATA

.... ❖ ....

....

PROJECT OVERVIEW

PART NAME: _____

PART NUMBER: _____

MATERIAL: _____

MACHINING DETAILS

MACHINE: _____

PROGRAM NO: _____

_____

REQUIREMENTS / CLAMPING

_____

_____

_____

MEASURING TOOLS AND OTHER COMMENTS

_____

_____

_____

TOOLS

	TOOL NAME / INSERTS		TOOLING SYSTEMS		OFFSET / PARAMETERS	
1						☐
2						☐
3						☐
4						☐
5						☐
6						☐
7						☐
8						☐
9						☐
10						☐
11						☐
12						☐
13						☐
14						☐
15						☐

PROJECT DATA

..... ❖ .....

....

PROJECT OVERVIEW

PART NAME: _____

PART NUMBER: _____

MATERIAL: _____

MACHINING DETAILS

MACHINE: _____

PROGRAM NO: _____

_____

REQUIREMENTS / CLAMPING

_____

_____

_____

_____

MEASURING TOOLS AND OTHER COMMENTS

_____

_____

_____

_____

....

....

....

....

TOOLS

	TOOL NAME / INSERTS		TOOLING SYSTEMS		OFFSET / PARAMETERS	
1						☐
2						☐
3						☐
4						☐
5						☐
6						☐
7						☐
8						☐
9						☐
10						☐
11						☐
12						☐
13						☐
14						☐
15						☐

PROJECT DATA

•••••• ❖ ••••••

PROJECT OVERVIEW

PART NAME:

PART NUMBER:

MATERIAL:

MACHINING DETAILS

MACHINE:

PROGRAM NO:

REQUIREMENTS / CLAMPING

MEASURING TOOLS AND OTHER COMMENTS

TOOLS

	TOOL NAME / INSERTS		TOOLING SYSTEMS		OFFSET / PARAMETERS	
1						☐
2						☐
3						☐
4						☐
5						☐
6						☐
7						☐
8						☐
9						☐
10						☐
11						☐
12						☐
13						☐
14						☐
15						☐

PROJECT DATA

························ ❖ ········

··

PROJECT OVERVIEW

PART NAME:

PART NUMBER:

MATERIAL:

MACHINING DETAILS

MACHINE:

PROGRAM NO:

REQUIREMENTS / CLAMPING

MEASURING TOOLS AND OTHER COMMENTS

··

··

··

························

TOOLS

	TOOL NAME / INSERTS		TOOLING SYSTEMS		OFFSET / PARAMETERS	
1						☐
2						☐
3						☐
4						☐
5						☐
6						☐
7						☐
8						☐
9						☐
10						☐
11						☐
12						☐
13						☐
14						☐
15						☐

PROJECT DATA

•••••• ❖ ••••••

....

PROJECT OVERVIEW

PART NAME: _____

PART NUMBER: _____

MATERIAL: _____

MACHINING DETAILS

MACHINE: _____

PROGRAM NO: _____

_____

REQUIREMENTS / CLAMPING

_____

_____

_____

_____

MEASURING TOOLS AND OTHER COMMENTS

_____

_____

_____

_____

....

....

....

TOOLS

	TOOL NAME / INSERTS		TOOLING SYSTEMS		OFFSET / PARAMETERS	
1						☐
2						☐
3						☐
4						☐
5						☐
6						☐
7						☐
8						☐
9						☐
10						☐
11						☐
12						☐
13						☐
14						☐
15						☐

PROJECT DATA

•••••• ❖ ••••••

....

PROJECT OVERVIEW

PART NAME: _____

PART NUMBER: _____

MATERIAL: _____

MACHINING DETAILS

MACHINE: _____

PROGRAM NO: _____

_____

REQUIREMENTS / CLAMPING

_____

_____

_____

_____

MEASURING TOOLS AND OTHER COMMENTS

_____

_____

_____

_____

TOOLS

	TOOL NAME / INSERTS		TOOLING SYSTEMS		OFFSET / PARAMETERS	
1						
2						
3						
4						
5						
6						
7						
8						
9						
10						
11						
12						
13						
14						
15						

PROJECT DATA

•••••• ❖ ••••••

PROJECT OVERVIEW

PART NAME:

PART NUMBER:

MATERIAL:

MACHINING DETAILS

MACHINE:

PROGRAM NO:

REQUIREMENTS / CLAMPING

MEASURING TOOLS AND OTHER COMMENTS

TOOLS

	TOOL NAME / INSERTS		TOOLING SYSTEMS		OFFSET / PARAMETERS	
1						☐
2						☐
3						☐
4						☐
5						☐
6						☐
7						☐
8						☐
9						☐
10						☐
11						☐
12						☐
13						☐
14						☐
15						☐

PROJECT DATA

•••••• ✜ ••••••

....

PROJECT OVERVIEW

PART NAME:

PART NUMBER:

MATERIAL:

MACHINING DETAILS

MACHINE:

PROGRAM NO:

REQUIREMENTS / CLAMPING

MEASURING TOOLS AND OTHER COMMENTS

TOOLS

	TOOL NAME / INSERTS		TOOLING SYSTEMS		OFFSET / PARAMETERS	
1						☐
2						☐
3						☐
4						☐
5						☐
6						☐
7						☐
8						☐
9						☐
10						☐
11						☐
12						☐
13						☐
14						☐
15						☐

PROJECT DATA

•••••• ✤ ••••••

PROJECT OVERVIEW

PART NAME:

PART NUMBER:

MATERIAL:

MACHINING DETAILS

MACHINE:

PROGRAM NO:

REQUIREMENTS / CLAMPING

MEASURING TOOLS AND OTHER COMMENTS

TOOLS

	TOOL NAME / INSERTS		TOOLING SYSTEMS		OFFSET / PARAMETERS	
1						☐
2						☐
3						☐
4						☐
5						☐
6						☐
7						☐
8						☐
9						☐
10						☐
11						☐
12						☐
13						☐
14						☐
15						☐

PROJECT DATA

.... ❖ ....

....

PROJECT OVERVIEW

PART NAME: _____

PART NUMBER: _____

MATERIAL: _____

MACHINING DETAILS

MACHINE: _____

PROGRAM NO: _____

_____

REQUIREMENTS / CLAMPING

_____

_____

_____

_____

MEASURING TOOLS AND OTHER COMMENTS

_____

_____

_____

_____

TOOLS

	TOOL NAME / INSERTS		TOOLING SYSTEMS		OFFSET / PARAMETERS	
1						☐
2						☐
3						☐
4						☐
5						☐
6						☐
7						☐
8						☐
9						☐
10						☐
11						☐
12						☐
13						☐
14						☐
15						☐

PROJECT DATA

········ ❖ ········

PROJECT OVERVIEW

PART NAME:

PART NUMBER:

MATERIAL:

MACHINING DETAILS

MACHINE:

PROGRAM NO:

REQUIREMENTS / CLAMPING

MEASURING TOOLS AND OTHER COMMENTS

TOOLS

	TOOL NAME / INSERTS		TOOLING SYSTEMS		OFFSET / PARAMETERS	
1						☐
2						☐
3						☐
4						☐
5						☐
6						☐
7						☐
8						☐
9						☐
10						☐
11						☐
12						☐
13						☐
14						☐
15						☐

PROJECT DATA

••••••• ❖ •••••••

....

PROJECT OVERVIEW

PART NAME:

PART NUMBER:

MATERIAL:

MACHINING DETAILS

MACHINE:

PROGRAM NO:

REQUIREMENTS / CLAMPING

MEASURING TOOLS AND OTHER COMMENTS

TOOLS

	TOOL NAME / INSERTS		TOOLING SYSTEMS		OFFSET / PARAMETERS	
1						☐
2						☐
3						☐
4						☐
5						☐
6						☐
7						☐
8						☐
9						☐
10						☐
11						☐
12						☐
13						☐
14						☐
15						☐

PROJECT DATA

PROJECT OVERVIEW

PART NAME:

PART NUMBER:

MATERIAL:

MACHINING DETAILS

MACHINE:

PROGRAM NO:

REQUIREMENTS / CLAMPING

MEASURING TOOLS AND OTHER COMMENTS

TOOLS

	TOOL NAME / INSERTS		TOOLING SYSTEMS		OFFSET / PARAMETERS	
1						☐
2						☐
3						☐
4						☐
5						☐
6						☐
7						☐
8						☐
9						☐
10						☐
11						☐
12						☐
13						☐
14						☐
15						☐

PROJECT DATA

.... ❖ ....

....

PROJECT OVERVIEW

PART NAME: _____

PART NUMBER: _____

MATERIAL: _____

MACHINING DETAILS

MACHINE: _____

PROGRAM NO: _____

_____

REQUIREMENTS / CLAMPING

_____

_____

_____

_____

MEASURING TOOLS AND OTHER COMMENTS

_____

_____

_____

_____

TOOLS

	TOOL NAME / INSERTS		TOOLING SYSTEMS		OFFSET / PARAMETERS	
1						☐
2						☐
3						☐
4						☐
5						☐
6						☐
7						☐
8						☐
9						☐
10						☐
11						☐
12						☐
13						☐
14						☐
15						☐

THANKS FOR YOUR PURCHASE AND SUPPORT

LEAVE A COMMENT AND RATING.

**IF YOU FIND THIS DIARY HELPFUL,
PLEASE SHARE IT WITH OTHERS.**

THIS WILL HELP US CREATE MORE PROJECTS

IF YOU NEED MORE STUFF CHECK AUTHOR:

CNC ASSIST

ON AMAZON

Galas Products

★★★★★

General Turning Formulas and Definitions
Values
Metric / Imperial

Cutting speed	$V_C = \dfrac{D_m \times \pi \times n}{1000}$ / $V_C = \dfrac{D_m \times \pi \times n}{12}$

Spindle speed	$n = \dfrac{V_C \times 1000}{n \times D_m}$ / $n = \dfrac{V_C \times 12}{n \times D_m}$

Metal removal rate	$Q = V_C \times a_p \times f_n$ / $Q = V_C \times a_p \times 12$

Net power	$P_C = \dfrac{V_C \times a_p \times f_n \times k_c}{60 \times 10^2}$ / $P_C = \dfrac{V_C \times a_p \times f_n \times k_c}{33 \times 10^2}$

Period of engagement	$T_C = \dfrac{l_m}{f_n \times n}$ / $T_C = \dfrac{l_m}{f_n \times n}$

SYMBOL	DESIGNATION/DEFINATION	UNIT, METRIC (IMPERIAL)
D_M	Machined diameter	mm (inch)
f_N	Feed per revolution	mm/r (inch/r)
a_P	Cutting depth	mm (inch)
V_C	Cutting speed	m/min (feet/min)
n	Spindle speed	rpm
P_C	Net power	kW (HP)
Q	Metal removal rate	cm^3/min ($inch^3$/min)
T_C	Period of engagement	min

General Milling Formulas and Definitions
Values
Metric / Imperial

Cutting speed	$V_C = \dfrac{DC_{ap} \times \pi \times n}{1000}$ / $V_C = \dfrac{DC_{ap} \times \pi \times n}{12}$

Spindle speed	$n = \dfrac{V_C \times 1000}{n \times DC_{ap}}$ / $n = \dfrac{V_C \times 12}{n \times DC_{ap}}$

Feed per tooth	$f_z = \dfrac{V_f}{n \times ZEFF}$ / $f_z = \dfrac{V_f}{n \times ZEFF}$

Feed per revolution	$f_n = \dfrac{V_f}{n}$ / $f_n = \dfrac{V_f}{n}$

Metal removal rate	$Q = V_C \times a_p \times f_n$ / $Q = V_C \times a_p \times 12$

Net power	$P_C = \dfrac{V_C \times a_p \times f_n \times k_c}{60 \times 10^2}$ / $P_C = \dfrac{V_C \times a_p \times f_n \times k_c}{33 \times 10^2}$

SYMBOL	DESIGNATION/DEFINITION	METRIC	IMPERIAL
A_P	Axial depth of cut	mm	inch
DC_{AP}	Cutting diam. at cutting depth ap	mm	inch
f_z	Feed per tooth	mm	inch
f_N	Feed per revolution	mm/r	inch
n	Spindle speed	rpm	rpm
V_C	Cutting speed	m/min	ft/min
Z_C	Number of effective teeth	pcs	pcs
P_C	Net power	kW	HP
Q	Metal removal rate	cm³/min	inch³/min
DC	Cutting diameter	mm	inch

Workpiece material groups

ISO P – Steel is the largest material group.. Machinability is usually good, but a lot depending on material hardness.

ISO M – Stainless steels are materials alloyed with a chromium. Other alloys may include molybdenum and nickel. Among all these materials the cutting edges are exposed to a great deal of heat, notch wear and built-up edge.

ISO K – Cast iron. Contrary to steel, a short-chipping type of material.
- Grey cast irons (GCI)
- Malleable cast irons (MCI)
- Nodular cast irons (NCI)
- Compact cast irons (CGI)
- Austempered cast irons (ADI)

All cast irons contain SiC, which is very abrasive to the cutting edge.

ISO N – Metals like aluminium, copper, brass etc. Aluminium with a Si-content of 13% is very abrasive. Generally, high cutting speeds and long tool life can be expected for inserts with sharp edges.

ISO S – Heat resistant super alloys include a great number of high-alloyed iron, nickel, cobalt and titanium based materials..They are very similar to the ISO M materials but are much more difficult to cut, and reduce the tool life of the insert edges.

ISO H – This group includes steels with a hardness between 45-65 HRc, and also chilled cast iron around 400-600 HB. The hardness makes them difficult to machine. The materials generate heat during cutting and are very abrasive for the cutting edge.

CNC *Turning insert shapes – simply guide*

R – Round
S – Square (90⁰)
C - 80⁰ diamond
W –Trigon (80⁰)
T – triangle (60⁰)
D - 55⁰ diamond
V - 35⁰ diamond

	R	S	C	W	T	D	V
Cutting edge strength	●	●	●	●	○	○	○
Stronger cutting edge	●	●	●	○	○	○	○
Higher feed rates	●	●	●	○	○	○	○
cutting force	●	●	●	○	○	○	○
vibration	●	●	●	●	○	○	○
accessibility	○	○	●	○	●	●	●

Depth of cut and cutting forces

- As a general rule of thumb, choose a nose radius that is equal or smaller than the depth of cut.

Positive or negative turning insert style

Positive insert	Negative insert
Single sided	Double and/or single sided
Low cutting forces	High edge strength
Side clearance	Zero clearance
First choice for internal turning and for external turning of slender components	First choice for external turning Heavy cutting conditions

G- CODES

CODE	DESCRIPTION	MILLING	TURNING
G00	Rapid positioning	M	T
G01	Linear interpolation	M	T
G02	Circular interpolation, clockwise	M	T
G03	Circular interpolation, counterclockwise	M	T
G04	Dwell	M	T
G07	Imaginary axis designation	M	
G09	Exact stop check, non-modal	M	T
G10	Programmable data input	M	T
G11	Data write cancel	M	T
G17	XY plane selection	M	
G18	ZX plane selection	M	T
G19	YZ plane selection	M	
G20	Programming in inches	M	T
G21	Programming in millimeters (mm)	M	T
G28	Return to home position	M	T
G30	Return to secondary home position	M	T
G31	Feed until skip function	M	
G32	Single-point threading, longhand style		T
G33	Constant-pitch threading	M	
G33	Single-point threading, longhand style		T
G34	Variable-pitch threading	M	
G40	Tool radius compensation off	M	T
G41	Tool radius compensation left	M	T
G42	Tool radius compensation right	M	T
G43	Tool height offset compensation negative	M	
G44	Tool height offset compensation positive	M	
G45	Axis offset single increase	M	
G46	Axis offset single decrease	M	
G47	Axis offset double increase	M	
G48	Axis offset double decrease	M	
G49	Tool length offset compensation cancel	M	
G50	Define the maximum spindle speed		T
G50	Scaling function cancel	M	
G50	Position register		T
G52	Local coordinate system (LCS)	M	
G53	Machine coordinate system	M	T

G- CODES

CODE	DESCRIPTION	MILLING	TURNING
G54	Work coordinate systems (WCSs)	M	T
G61	Exact stop check, modal	M	T
G62	Automatic corner override	M	T
G64	Default cutting mode	M	T
G68	Rotate coordinate system	M	
G69	Turn off coordinate system rotation	M	
G74	Peck drilling cycle for turning		T
G74	Tapping cycle for milling, lefthand thread, M04 spindle direction	M	
G75	Peck grooving cycle for turning		T
G76	Fine boring cycle for milling	M	
G76	Threading cycle for turning, multiple repetitive cycle		T
G80	Cancel canned cycle	M	T
G82	Drilling cycle with dwell	M	
G83	Peck drilling cycle	M	
G85	boring cycle, feed in/feed out	M	
G88	boring cycle, feed in/spindle stop/manual operation	M	
G89	boring cycle, feed in/dwell/feed out	M	
G90	Absolute programming	M	T (B)
G92	Position register	M	T (B)
G94	Fixed cycle, simple cycle, for roughing (X-axis emphasis)		T (A)
G95	Feedrate per revolution	M	T (B)
G96	Constant surface speed (CSS)		T
G97	Constant spindle speed	M	T
G98	Return to initial Z level in canned cycle	M	
G98	Feedrate per minute (group type A)		T (A)
G99	Return to R level in canned cycle	M	
G99	Feedrate per revolution (group type A)		T (A)
G100	Tool length measurement	M	

M-CODES

Code	Description	Milling	Turning
M00	Compulsory stop	M	T
M01	Optional stop	M	T
M02	End of program	M	T
M03	Spindle on (clockwise rotation)	M	T
M04	Spindle on (counterclockwise rotation)	M	T
M05	Spindle stop	M	T
M06	Automatic tool change (ATC)	M	T
M07	Coolant on (mist)	M	T
M08	Coolant on (flood)	M	T
M09	Coolant off	M	T
M10	Pallet clamp on	M	
M11	Pallet clamp off	M	
M13	Spindle on (clockwise rotation) and coolant on (flood)	M	
M19	Spindle orientation	M	T
M21	Mirror, X-axis	M	
M21	Tailstock forward		T
M22	Mirror, Y-axis	M	
M22	Tailstock backward		T
M23	Mirror OFF	M	
M23	Thread gradual pullout ON		T
M24	Thread gradual pullout OFF		T
M30	End of program, with return to program top	M	T
M41	Gear select – gear 1		T
M42	Gear select – gear 2		T
M43	Gear select – gear 3		T
M44	Gear select – gear 4		T
M48	Feedrate override allowed	M	T
M49	Feedrate override NOT allowed	M	T
M52	Unload Last tool from spindle	M	T
M60	Automatic pallet change (APC)	M	
M98	Subprogram call	M	T
M99	Subprogram end	M	T

Abbreviations used by programmers and operators

APC	AUTOMATIC PALLET CHANGER
ATC	automatic tool changer
CAD/CAM	computer-aided design and computer-aided manufacturing
CCW	counterclockwise
CNC	computerized numerical control
CRC	cutter radius compensation
CS	cutting speed
CSS	constant surface speed
CW	clockwise
DNC	direct numerical control or distributed numerical control
DOC	depth of cut
EOB	end of block
E-STOP	emergency stop
EXT	external
FIM	full indicator movement
FPM	feet per minute
HBM	horizontal boring mill
HMC	horizontal machining center
HSM	high speed machining
HSS	high speed steel
IN	inch(es)
IPF	inches per flute
IPM	inches per minute
IPR	inches per revolution
IPT	inches per tooth
MDI	manual data input
MEM	memory
MFO	manual feedrate override
MM	millimetre(s)
MPG	manual pulse generator
NC	numerical control
OSS	oriented spindle stop
SFM	surface feet per minute
SFPM	surface feet per minute
SPT	single-point threading
SSO	spindle speed override
TC OR T/C	tool change, tool changer
TIR	total indicator reading
TPI	threads per inch
USB	Universal Serial Bus
VMC	vertical machining center
VTL	vertical turret lathe

Dimensions of metric threads (60°)

M	P	Hole Ø min	Hole Ø max	Shaft Ø min	Shaft Ø max
M1	0.25	0.73	0.79	0.92	0.98
M1.2	0.25	0.93	0.98	1.11	1.18
M1.4	0.3	1.07	1.14	1.31	1.38
M1.6	0.35	1.22	1.32	1.50	1.58
M1.8	0.35	1.42	1.52	1.70	1.78
M2	0.4	1.57	1.68	1.89	1.98
M2.2	0.45	1.71	1.84	2.08	2.18
M2.5	0.45	2.01	2.14	2.38	2.48
M3	0.5	2.46	2.60	2.87	2.98
M3.5	0.6	2.85	3.01	3.35	3.48
M4	0.7	3.24	3.42	3.84	3.98
M4.5	0.75	3.69	3.88	4.34	4.48
M5	0.8	4.13	4.33	4.83	4.98
M6	1	4.92	5.15	5.79	5.97
M7	1	5.92	6.15	6.79	6.97
M8	1.25	6.65	6.91	7.76	7.97
M9	1.25	7.65	7.91	8.76	8.97
M10	1.5	8.38	8.68	9.73	9.97
M11	1.5	9.38	9.68	10.73	10.97
M12	1.75	10.11	10.44	11.70	11.97
M14	2	11.84	12.21	13.68	13.96
M16	2	13.84	14.21	15.68	15.96
M18	2.5	15.29	15.74	17.62	17.96
M20	2.5	17.29	17.74	19.62	19.96
M22	2.5	19.29	19.74	21.62	21.96
M24	3	20.75	21.25	23.58	23.95
M27	3	23.75	24.25	26.58	26.95
M30	3.5	26.21	26.77	29.52	29.95
M33	3.5	29.21	29.77	32.52	32.95
M36	4	31.67	32.27	35.47	35.94
M39	4	34.67	35.27	38.47	38.94
M42	4.5	37.13	37.80	41.44	41.94
M45	4.5	40.13	40.80	44.44	44.94

Dimensions of inch threads (55°)

G	1"/P	P [mm]	Hole DIA min	Hole DIA max	Shaft DIA min	Shaft DIA max
1/16	28	0.907	6.56	6.84	7.51	7.72
1/8	28	0.907	8.57	8.85	9.51	9.73
1/4	19	1.337	11.45	11.89	12.91	13.16
3/8	19	1.337	14.95	15.39	16.41	16.66
1/2	14	1.814	18.63	19.17	20.67	20.95
5/8	14	1.814	20.59	21.13	22.63	22.91
3/4	14	1.814	24.12	24.66	26.16	26.44
7/8	14	1.814	27.88	28.42	29.92	30.20
1	11	2.309	30.29	30.93	32.89	33.25
1 1/8	11	2.309	34.94	35.58	37.54	37.90
1 1/4	11	2.309	38.95	39.59	41.55	41.91
1 1/2	11	2.309	44.84	45.48	47.44	47.80
1 3/4	11	2.309	50.79	51.43	53.39	53.75
2	11	2.309	56.66	57.30	59.25	59.61
2 1/4	11	2.309	62.75	63.39	65.28	65.71
2 1/2	11	2.309	72.23	72.87	74.75	75.18
2 3/4	11	2.309	78.58	79.22	81.10	81.53
3	11	2.309	84.93	85.57	87.45	87.88
3 1/2	11	2.309	97.37	98.01	99.90	100.33
4	11	2.309	110.07	110.71	112.60	113.03
4 1/2	11	2.309	122.77	123.41	125.30	125.73
5	11	2.309	135.47	136.11	138.00	138.43
5 1/2	11	2.309	148.17	148.81	150.70	151.13
6	11	2.309	160.87	161.51	163.40	163.83

UNF - Unified National Fine Threads (60°)

MAJOR DIAMETER	THREADS PER INCH	MAJOR DIAMETER		PITCH
(in)	(tpi)	(in)	(mm)	(mm)
#0 - 80	80	0.060	1.524	0.317
#1 - 72	72	0.073	1.854	0.353
#2 - 64	64	0.086	2.184	0.397
#3 - 56	56	0.099	2.515	0.453
#4 - 48	48	0.112	2.845	0.529
#5 - 44	44	0.125	3.175	0.577
#6 - 40	40	0.138	3.505	0.635
#8 - 36	36	0.164	4.166	0.705
#10 - 32	32	0.190	4.826	0.794
#12 - 28	28	0.216	5.486	0.907
1/4" - 28	28	0.250	6.350	0.907
5/16" - 24	24	0.313	7.938	1.058
3/8" - 24	24	0.375	9.525	1.058
7/16" - 20	20	0.438	11.112	1.270
1/2" - 20	20	0.500	12.700	1.270
9/16" - 18	18	0.563	14.288	1.411
5/8" - 18	18	0.625	15.875	1.411
3/4" - 16	16	0.750	19.050	1.587
7/8" - 14	14	0.875	22.225	1.814
1" - 12	12	1.000	25.400	2.117
1 1/8" - 12	12	1.125	28.575	2.117
1 1/4" - 12	12	1.250	31.750	2.117
1 3/8" - 12	12	1.375	34.925	2.117
1 1/2" - 12	12	1.500	38.100	2.117

UNC - Unified Coarse Threads (60°)

Major Diameter	Threads per inch	Major Diameter		Pitch
(in)	(tpi)	(in)	(mm)	(mm)
#1 - 64	64	0.073	1.854	0.397
#2 - 56	56	0.086	2.184	0.453
#3 - 48	48	0.099	2.515	0.529
#4 - 40	40	0.112	2.845	0.635
#5 - 40	40	0.125	3.175	0.635
#6 - 32	32	0.138	3.505	0.794
#8 - 32	32	0.164	4.166	0.794
#10 - 24	24	0.190	4.826	1.058
#12 - 24	24	0.216	5.486	1.058
1/4" - 20	20	0.250	6.350	1.270
5/16" - 18	18	0.313	7.938	1.411
3/8" - 16	16	0.375	9.525	1.587
7/16" - 14	14	0.438	11.112	1.814
1/2" - 13	13	0.500	12.700	1.954
9/16" - 12	12	0.563	14.288	2.117
5/8" - 11	11	0.625	15.875	2.309
3/4" - 10	10	0.750	19.050	2.540
7/8" - 9	9	0.875	22.225	2.822
1" - 8	8	1.000	25.400	3.175
1 1/8" - 7	7	1.125	28.575	3.628
1 1/4" - 7	7	1.250	31.750	3.628
1 3/8" - 6	6	1.375	34.925	4.233
1 1/2" - 6	6	1.500	38.100	4.233
1 3/4" - 5	5	1.750	44.450	5.080
2" - 4 1/2	4 1/2	2.000	50.800	5.644
2 1/4" - 4 1/2	4 1/2	2.250	57.150	5.644
2 1/2" - 4	4	2.500	63.500	6.350
2 3/4" - 4	4	2.750	69.850	6.350
3" - 4	4	3.000	76.200	6.350
3 1/4" - 4	4	3.250	82.550	6.350
3 1/2" - 4	4	3.500	88.900	6.350
3 3/4" - 4	4	3.750	95.250	6.350
4" - 4	4	4.000	101.600	6.350

Hardness Comparision

Brinell HB	Vickers HV	Rockwell C HRC	Rockwell B HRB	Leeb HLD
800	-	72	-	856
780	1220	71	-	850
760	1210	70	-	843
745	1114	68	-	837
725	1060	67	-	829
712	1021	66	-	824
682	940	65	-	812
668	905	64	-	806
652	867	63	-	799
626	803	62	-	787
614	775	61	-	782
601	746	60	-	776
590	727	59	-	770
576	694	57	-	763
552	649	56	-	751
545	639	55	-	748
529	606	54	-	739
514	587	53	120	731
502	565	52	119	724
495	551	51	119	719
477	534	49	118	709
461	502	48	117	699
451	489	47	117	693
444	474	46	116	688
427	460	45	115	677
415	435	44	115	669
401	423	43	114	660
388	401	42	114	650
375	390	41	113	640
370	385	40	112	635
362	380	39	111	630
351	361	38	111	622
346	352	37	110	617
341	344	37	110	613
331	335	36	109	605
323	320	35	109	599
311	312	34	108	588
301	305	33	107	579
293	291	32	106	572
285	285	31	105	565
276	278	30	105	557
269	272	29	104	550
261	261	28	103	542
258	258	27	102	539
249	250	25	101	530
245	246	24	100	526
240	240	23	99	521
237	235	23	99	518
229	226	22	98	510
224	221	21	97	505
217	217	20	96	497
211	213	19	95	491
206	209	18	94	485
203	201	17	94	482
200	199	16	93	478
196	197	15	92	474